W9-COL-845

how to **choose wine**

how to choose wine

a complete guide to buying,
storing, and serving wine

MITCHELL BEAZLEY

susy atkins

how to choose wine

by susy atkins

First published in Great Britain in 2002
by Mitchell Beazley, an imprint of Octopus
Publishing Group Limited, 2–4 Heron Quays,
London E14 4JP.

Reprinted 2002

Copyright © Octopus Publishing Group
Ltd 2002
Text copyright © Susy Atkins 2002

All rights reserved. No part of this work may
be reproduced or utilized in any form or by
any means, electronic or mechanical, including
photocopying, recording or by any information
storage and retrieval system, without the prior
written permission of the publishers.

A CIP catalogue record for this book is
available from the British Library.

ISBN: 1 84000 577 7

The author and publishers will be grateful
for any information which will assist them in
keeping future editions up to date. Although
all reasonable care has been taken in the
preparation of this book, neither the publishers
nor the author can accept any liability for any
consequences arising from the use thereof,
or the information contained therein.

Commissioning editor   Rebecca Spry
Executive art editor   Yasia Williams
Photographer   Alan Williams
Managing editor   Emma Rice
Design   Nicky Collings
Editor   Gill Pitts
Production   Alix McCulloch
Index   John Noble

Mitchell Beazley would like to thank Denbies
Wine Estate, Surrey and Majestic Wine
Warehouse, Chalk Farm and Docklands for the
use of their premises for the photography.

Typeset in RotisSansSerif

Printed and bound by
Toppan Printing Company in China

contents

introduction

A little information on wine goes a long way – although to hear some connoisseurs you'd think you had to be a Master of Wine just to pick a bottle off a shelf. Rubbish! If you understand the basics about grape varieties, countries, and some of the main issues such as oaking, pricing, food matching, and storing, then you can a) avoid the nasty bottles lurking out there, and b) get a great deal more out of the liquid in your glass. This book aims to give you a head start, explaining in straightforward language how to pick a wine that suits each occasion, from weddings to dinner parties to inexpensive everyday drinking. At the end of the day, no one should tell anyone else exactly which wine to choose. But I'm confident that the facts, hints, and general guidelines contained here will help steer you towards wine that suits you and your individual taste. And you never know: it might start something and inspire you to find out a whole lot more in the future. Happy drinking!

finding a wine you like

Get to grips with grape varieties and the fascinating
array of flavours and aromas they produce, and you
will suddenly know an awful lot more about wine.
Here's your guide to the essential grape varieties, plus
the lowdown on the names of specific styles and tips
for buying wine on a budget or for special occasions.

It's essential to understand the important grape varieties and the styles of wine they produce. But there are other factors at play which determine the character of the stuff in your glass. Here are three of them.

three key wine issues

Old World vs New World

Ten years ago it was usually clear whether a wine came from the New World (Australia, Chile, California...) or from the Old World (Europe). New World wine was ripe, fruity, and squeaky clean, the result of high-tech winemaking, while Old World versions were probably more interesting and complex, but more likely to show faults. European winemakers used to place emphasis on "terroir", the character of individual vineyards, while for the new kids on the block, wine could be crafted to order as long as the equipment and viticulture were up to date.

Today, you may have difficulty distinguishing New World wine from Old. Why? Winemakers increasingly agree that terroir *and* modern winemaking together make fine wine. Old World winemakers are creating fruitier, cleaner wines, while the New World is placing more emphasis on regions and even individual vineyard sites. Today, a rich, oaky white labelled Clearwater Valley Chardonnay could easily come from Hungary or the Languedoc, South Africa or Chile.

Blends vs single varieties

Once you've discovered a grape variety you like, it's tempting to stick with it and ignore the other options. Don't get stuck in a rut, as there are so many other flavours and aromas to sample. That goes for combinations of grapes too. It's a myth that single-varietal wines (one hundred per cent Chardonnay or one hundred per cent Merlot, for example) are always better than blends, although they have been more fashionable recently. In fact, many of the world's greatest wines are blends, and it can be argued that these are more complex and exciting than those made from just one variety.

Take Cabernet Sauvignon/Merlot blends, for example. Most top clarets are made mainly from a blend of these two grape varieties. The Cabernet provides structure, power, and a wonderful cassis character, while the Merlot component fleshes out the wine with its generous, plummy fruit and soft, ripe flavours. Grassy, crisp Sauvignon Blanc and fatter, honeyed Semillon are also often blended together in southwest France, sometimes with brilliant results. The Australians have made powerful, compelling blends of Cabernet and spicy Shiraz, while many of the best sparkling wines in the world are created by splicing the juice of Chardonnay with that of Pinot Noir.

Keep an open mind when choosing your wine and try both single-varietal wines and blends.

Vintages: do you need to know?

In every winemaking region, each harvest is different from the last, so mug up on the best years – especially if a) you intend to buy expensive, fine wine or b) you want to cellar it for any length of time.

Most of us have heard of the grapes Cabernet Sauvignon, Merlot, and Pinot Noir. But have you tasted Nebbiolo, Malbec, or Zinfandel? Throw open the door to other red varieties and experience some exciting new flavours and styles.

the great red grapes

Super stoppers

It used to be a very bad sign if your wine was bottled in anything other than glass with a natural cork. Not so today. Screw caps can be found on good-quality wines, especially Australian ones, and plastic corks have been adopted by many progressive modern wineries. It seems a lot of us are simply fed up with the huge amount of (natural) cork taint. Even wine boxes seem to contain more palatable booze these days.

Cabernet Sauvignon

Imagine a deep rich colour, ripe blackcurrant flavour, firm structure, and aromatic hints of cedar and chocolate. Mature wines have mellow, gamey flavours and a cigar-box aroma. Cabernet is rightly respected. Often blended with Merlot and Cabernet Franc in Bordeaux (to make claret), Shiraz in Australia, or Sangiovese in Italy.

Also try:

Nebbiolo – makes firm, powerful Barolo and Barbaresco.
Tempranillo – Rioja's traditionally oaky reds with ripe strawberry and vanilla character.

Pinot Noir

A smoothie, Pinot is behind silky, soft, beguiling wines with seductive red-berry flavours. With age, these can become earthy, with a manure-like aroma (better than it sounds). Most red burgundy is Pinot Noir; some great examples too, from California, New Zealand, and cooler parts of Australia. Can be unreliable and expensive, so tread carefully.

Also try:
Gamay – the Beaujolais grape, producing less serious but often juicy, appealing reds that smell like summer pudding.
Cabernet Franc – raspberry-scented, slightly grassy reds from the Loire Valley. Try them chilled.

Syrah/Shiraz
Fashionable Syrah is behind many of the spicy wines of the Rhône Valley and, as Shiraz, it produces powerful, blockbuster Aussie reds. Not overtly fruity, it often smells and tastes of cloves, chocolate, leather, and black pepper.

Also try:
Grenache – often blended with Syrah, but on its own it makes fruitier reds in Spain, southern France, and Australia.
Zinfandel – raspberry and black pepper from California.

Merlot
Fleshy, generously fruity reds majoring on sweetly ripe plum, redcurrant, and chocolate flavours, Merlot is often blended with Cabernet (in Bordeaux), providing gentle lushness. Trendy in the New World as a single-varietal wine, the best hailing from Chile, California, South Africa.

Also try:
Sangiovese – tangy strawberries, a hint of herbs and tobacco, this grape makes seriously good wines, notably Chianti.
Malbec – plenty of black-cherry fruit, usually medium-bodied but smooth, produces Argentina's most exciting reds.

Does region matter?
A particular grape variety does not taste the same the world over, and one crucial factor in this is region – climate and soil in particular. For example, red wine from a hot region, such as the Languedoc in southern France, tends to taste a lot riper and richer than red wine from a cooler spot, such as the Loire, even if it is made from the same variety. Increasingly, winemakers across the globe are realizing that they can't just make a wine the way they want it; they have to respect the origins of the grapes and the natural character this gives the wine.

Tired of Chardonnay? It comes in many different guises, so don't give up on it. That said, it's well worth casting around for some white wines made from other grapes. Here are some of the main rivals for your affections.

the great white grapes

Dry vs sweet

Back in the 1970s medium-sweet whites were fashionable, then bone-dry styles took over. Today, thankfully, anything goes. Problems arise, however, when it isn't clear from the label whether a wine is sweet, medium, or dry. Wines from Alsace are notoriously difficult in this respect, and white Bordeaux has been known to flummox drinkers too. *See* the label glossary on page 62 for some guidance, but trial and error can sometimes be the only solution.

Chardonnay

Chardonnay has taken over the world, stealing the hearts of winemakers everywhere. But not all wine drinkers feel the same – many Chardonnays are over-oaked and overblown. The ripest and most powerful ones come from hotter parts of California and Australia. More elegant styles are made in Chablis and Italy, while New Zealand and South Africa produce medium-weight contenders. Chile, Eastern Europe, Argentina, and southern France score for great value, but top burgundies rule – complex and full of nuts, cream, apples....

Also try:

Viognier – it's peachy, man. Fleshy, floral-scented wines oozing peach and apricot from the Rhône or the New World.

Semillon – younger versions are grassy and lean, but with age the wines become fatter, lime-juicy, and honeyed.

Albariño – western Spain's acclaimed white grape makes scented, tangy, and ripe wines for matching with fish.

Chenin Blanc – tastes of apples and smells of hay.... Good Chenin is lovely stuff, but poor examples abound.

Riesling

Don't make the mistake of equating Riesling with the worst cheap German whites (which are made from inferior grapes). Riesling makes some of the world's best whites. Think apples and pears, delicate orchard-fruit flavours, spine-tingling acidity when young, with softer, richer honey, and even petrol aromas creeping in with age; it keeps for years.

Also try:

Gewurztraminer – Gewurz has an exotic aroma of rose petals, ginger, lychees, and Turkish Delight. **Pinot Blanc** – no one could argue with such a pleasant wine: fresh, soft, and appley and highly quaffable.
Pinot Gris/Grigio – Gris is richer, with a golden colour and smoky, spicy hints. Italian Pinot Grigio is lighter, spritzier.

Sauvignon Blanc

Now very fashionable, whether you prefer the elegant lemons-and-grapefruit style from the Loire, or the deeply aromatic, succulent wines bursting with gooseberry and tomato leaf from New Zealand. Blended with Semillon in Southwest France to create grassy whites both mundane and marvellous. Almost always unoaked (except in California).

Also try:

Muscat – wines made from this grape actually taste of, um, grapes: crunchy green ones. A tangy, mouth-watering variety.
Muscadet – a neutral white wine, but zippy and fresh and perfect for washing down shellfish.

To oak or not to oak

White wine aged carefully in oak barrels has an added complexity, structure, and richness, and often displays rich notes of vanilla, butter, toast, and spice.... A talented winemaker can get the oak to meld with the natural flavour of the wine, and aims to create the right balance between oak, fruit, acidity, and so on. Some whites really do benefit from oak, and would seem bland and one-dimensional without it. But clumsy, over-oaked whites are out there; avoid those which smell and taste like sawdust and vanilla essence. Only a termite could enjoy such wines, which are often made by dunking oak chips in the wine.

Some of the most exciting wines in the world are either sweet or fortified (with spirit, usually); they offer opulent flavours and aromas. And here are the crucial facts on fizz.

sparkling, sweet, & fortified

Low alcohol = bad wine?

Wines which are naturally low in alcohol taste enormously better than wines that are deliberately made to be light in alcohol, or alcohol-free. Fine German Riesling often weighs in at around just nine per cent alcohol (compared with fourteen per cent for many New World whites), while the less serious but delightfully refreshing Moscato d'Asti has even less. "Alcohol-free" wine usually disappoints.

Chardonnay

Chardonnay has its tendrils in every nook and cranny, including Champagne, where it is one of three grapes that can be used for arguably the best bubbly in the world. It is also used to make sparklers in other French regions and the New World, and even pops up in some modern cavas.

Pinot Noir

Another of the grapes used in Champagne, Pinot Noir is prized for its red-berry fragrance and fruitiness. It is used to make fine fizz in other parts of France and in the New World, where it is almost always blended with Chardonnay.

Pinot Meunier

The third Champagne grape, Pinot Meunier contributes a lively, fresh, and fruity quality to the blend.

Also try:
Riesling – racy, crisp German, Austrian, and Alsace fizz.
Xarel-lo, Parellada, and Macabeo – what a mouthful!
The Spanish grapes that make easy-drinking, appley cava.

Moscato Bianco (Muscat) – used to make Asti and
Moscato d'Asti in Italy, Clairette in southern France.
Shiraz – in the fun form of curranty, frothy reds from Oz.

Palomino Fino

Palomino produces dull table wine but magnificent sherry.
Fino, manzanilla, amontillado, oloroso – all are made almost
entirely from Palomino vines grown in Spain's Jerez region.

Touriga Nacional

Port is made from a blend of different grapes, but Touriga
forms the core of many of the greatest bottles. The small,
tough-skinned berries produce a deep colour, lots of tannin,
and an intense aroma and flavour of red berries.

Muscat

The Muscat family makes a great deal of the sweet wine
produced around the world, from light, lemony Moscatel
de Valencia to honeyed, floral scented French *vins doux
naturels* and gloopy, toffeed Aussie liqueur Muscats.

Not forgetting:

Semillon/Sauvignon – responsible for France's great "nobly
rotten" (botrytized) dessert wines, Sauternes and Barsac.
Riesling – also creates superb, complex, sweet wine with
crisp acidity, mainly from Germany, Canada, Austria.
Furmint – the grape which, when nobly rotten, is behind
Hungary's marmalade, honey, and peach-flavoured Tokáji,
one of the world's most luscious dessert wines.

What is noble rot?

Botrytis cinerea, aka noble
rot, attacks a ripe grape,
making it shrivel and
concentrating the flavours.
The wines that are made
from botrytis-affected
grapes are unusually
gloopy, with naturally high
sugar levels, well preserved
acidity, and a delicious
character of beeswax,
honey, and barley sugar.

Don't listen to anyone who says you can never find a decent bottle of cut-price white, a palatable mid-price claret, or a tasty sparkler without breaking the bank. If you find something you really like at a particularly low price, good for you. That said, some general advice is useful in determining which wines offer the best value for money, so what follows is not set in stone, but a general set of guidelines:

sticking to a budget

Big brands

By all means, stick to wine made by well-known major producers if you like, as these bottles tend to be fairly safe and reliable. But the big wine brands also tend to be fairly bland – they are crowd-pleasers not thought-provokers. In general, it pays to seek out smaller producers and rarer labels for more individual styles and flavours.

Bargain basement
Whites

Chardonnay from Chile, South of France, Eastern Europe – soft, buttery, and ripe.
Touraine Sauvignon Blanc – better value than rest of the Loire.
Vin de Pays des Côtes de Gascogne – dry, grassy, and lemony.
German Riesling – a rare bargain can be found.
Hungary – spicy whites and Sauvignons can be tasty.
Avoid: German hock, Liebfraumilch, Piesporter.

Reds

Portugal – modern, fruity reds from the central regions.
Southern Italy and Sicily – unusual flavours from local grapes.
South of France – ripe, rich but soft red wines.
Chile and Argentina – great value Cabernet and Merlot.
Spain – the cheapest Spanish reds are much improved.
Avoid: Beaujolais Nouveau and claret.

Sparkling and others

Cava – Spain's wonderfully inexpensive, fresh, snappy fizz.

Asti/Moscato d'Asti – sweet and frothy, great with dessert.

Sherry – don't turn your nose up at own-label sherry, which is often ludicrously underpriced.

Rosés - fresh, young, appealing rosé from France and Spain is usually competively priced.

Mid-priced gems

Whites

New Zealand Sauvignon and Chardonnay – wonderfully pure, zesty fruit flavours and crisp acidity.

Loire – discover elegant Sauvignon, complex Chenin Blanc.

Australia – try Riesling, Semillon, and Verdelho as well as the ubiquitous Chardonnay.

Chile – whites are better value in the mid-priced range.

Italy – food-friendly whites from the centre, east, and north (fine Soave, Lugana, Arneis).

South Africa – top Chardonnays are remarkably good value.

Avoid: Overblown, over-oaked Californian whites and most white burgundy (sorry, you'll still have to pay more...).

Reds

Chile and Argentina – excellent Cabernet, Merlot, Malbec.

Tuscany – some fascinating flavours start to creep in.

Rhône – concentrated, spicy, and firm structure.

Australia – reigns supreme in this bracket for ripe reds.

South Africa – single varietals and blends from Stellenbosch and Paarl areas can be stunning.

**Half-bottles
and magnums**

Size does count.
Half-bottles make sense
when you only sip a little
at a time yet want to make
sure you crack open a fresh
bottle regularly, while
magnums (the volume of
two ordinary bottles) look
exciting at parties. You
shouldn't pay significantly
more or less to buy in
magnums, although
half-bottles can be a tad
more pricey, glass for glass.

Avoid: claret and burgundy – still dodgy.
Eastern Europe – not competitive at this price point.

Sparkling and others

New World premium fizz – especially from New Zealand.
Vintage cava – more depth of flavour than non-vintage.
Crémants – France's best sparklers after Champagne.
Fortified wines – port can be reasonably good value at
this price, as can serious sherries (dry oloroso, PX).
Avoid: the cheapest Champagnes – lean, mean and green.

Worth splashing out on

Many higher priced wines are good – but only some are
wonderful. What should you splash out on? This is where
claret (red Bordeaux) and Burgundy start to get really
interesting, so it's worth saving up for the pricier bottles.
Champagne too, begins to impress as you spend more
although you have to spend a lot to get the best vintage
Champers. The serious but sensible money is also on top
German and Austrian Rieslings, fine Loire whites (dry and
sweet) and the reputable dessert wines from Bordeaux
(Sauternes), Austria and Hungary (Tokáji). Vintage ports
and mature Madeiras are "must-haves" for a real treat.
Avoid: many critics believe the New World can't compete
at the top as the wines lack finesse and complexity when
tasted beside Europe's best. It is probably true to say
that the New World is more competitive at lower prices,
although the very finest wines of Australia and California
in particular are world-class and merit a high price tag.

The golden rule before buying wine in large quantities for a special occasion is "taste before you buy". Why not invest in several different bottles and have a fun tasting session at home? You'll be glad you spent a little time and money working out which ones are best for your bash.

buying for occasions

Weddings

No, you don't have to buy expensive, flashy Champagne for weddings. A fresh sparkling wine will often go down just as well, if not better, than an inferior and harshly acidic Champagne. Instead, pick a lively, fruity, easy-drinking fizz from California, New Zealand, or Australia, or a quality sparkler, such as crémant, from another region of France.

However, if you can be sure you've bagged a decent one, there's nothing quite like Champagne for finesse and kudos. If you do decide to splash out on the Real McCoy, go for a well-known, reliable non-vintage brand or a vintage Champagne (but make sure it is mature – avoid the youngest on the shelves.)

Perhaps the best solution (and the one I went for at my own wedding) is to invest in a few bottles of a special and splendid vintage Champagne for the toast, and case-loads of a fun, frivolous New World fizz for the rest of the party.

How much per person?

Cater for too much rather than too little – if you buy sale or return you won't lose out. Aim for a bottle per head if you are holding a boozy drinks party, or half a bottle per head for an elegant dinner. Wedding guests tend to drink a huge amount – especially if the party lasts all day and evening – so stock up well!

Wine with food

There are no hard and fast rules in food and wine matching. If you like a rich red with your grilled trout, then fine. Still, general guidelines can be helpful. Think about all the ingredients in the dish, not just the main one, and find a wine to match the whole plateful. And try to find similar levels of sweetness, acidity, weight, and power in your food and wine so that the wine doesn't overpower the dish or vice versa. Finally, think of the wine like a sauce: red-berry flavours go with lamb; lemony flavours with fish, and so on.

Table wines for the wedding feast should be crowd-pleasers; soft, fruity, and fresh. Ripe vin de pays d'Oc, Rhône reds, or decent Australian blends will do the trick and go well with a wide variety of dishes. This is perhaps not the moment to wheel out a new-wave Chardonnay called Fat Geezer, or a wine box with "cut-price Lambrusco" emblazoned on it. Choose something that looks reasonably sophisticated.

Dinner parties

Obviously, it depends what you are serving, but in most cases stock up with a dry white or fizz to act as an aperitif, more white as well as red for the dinner itself (always offer both), and something a bit different, such as a dessert wine or port (or both) for the pudding/cheese and afterwards. It's a clever idea to choose one white or fizz that works well as an aperitif and matches your food: for example, a light Chablis that you can serve as guests arrive and take through to the table to match the smoked salmon.

Trade up a bit from your usual, everyday bottles – there's no point in cooking fabulous food only to wash it down with nasty cheap plonk. Aim to spend just two or three pounds more per bottle to get much better quality, and don't forget to use palatable wine in the cooking. Never use the dregs from your last dinner party three months ago.

Wines that are particularly food friendly include:
Whites: Pinot Blanc from Alsace, lightly oaked or

unoaked Chardonnay, and fine German Riesling.
Reds: New World Merlot, young Pinot Noir, Rioja Reserva,
Chianti Classico, and mature claret.

Drinks parties
Unless you are desperately trying to impress, a drinks party
should be fuelled by bargain wines: straightforward, tasty
bottles which most people will enjoy. A list of good-value
bargain basement wines appears on page 18. Without food,
you won't need heavy, tannic reds, so choose lighter styles,
and avoid whites that are extremely tart or on the sweeter
side, or have been heavily oaked. Wines with enormous
character can be savoured properly another time, so stick
to well-balanced crowd-pleasers which slip down easily.

Top of your shopping list for party wines should be:
Spanish cava – great-value fizz, and the perfect base for
sparkling cocktails.
Light, fruity, unoaked whites – try South African Chenin
Blanc, New World Sauvignon Blanc, Spanish whites from
the Rueda region....
Soft, juicy, easy going reds – try a bargain from Portugal,
a Chilean Merlot or Pinot Noir, a good quality Beaujolais,
an Argentinian Bonarda....
Finally, don't forget wine boxes and bottles with screw caps
(*see* page 12) for ease of opening.

The countries

Argentina

Some very appealing, ripe, and modern reds are now emerging from Argentina. Don't miss the smooth, concentrated, black-cherry-flavoured Malbecs, only rivalled by the more serious Cabernets and Syrahs. Wines made from the Bonarda grape provide juicy, soft, everyday reds.

red wines a–z

Australia

As we all know, Australian reds have moved from being a national joke to some of the most critically acclaimed wines around. In general, expect fruit-driven, ripe, and fairly powerful styles. Although the inexpensive big brands, especially the cross-regional blends, are reliable, they are usually one-dimensional and their simple fruitiness soon gets boring. It pays to explore the country's regional styles and seek out the more characterful wines – Aussie reds are better value at the middle- and top end of the market. Start by trying Shiraz from the Barossa or Hunter valleys, Cabernet from Coonawarra, and Pinot Noir from Victoria's Yarra Valley.

Bulgaria

Great-value Bulgarian Cabernet and Merlot stormed the shelves in the 1980s, but made less impact in the 1990s as the newly privatized wine industry fell into disarray and New World countries came up with the goods. Now Bulgaria is beginning to fight back with more competitive wines. Tread carefully and you may well unearth a new-wave bargain. Doesn't compete in the top price brackets.

Chile

With its wonderfully pure cassis flavour and fair price, it's hard to beat Chilean Cabernet. Merlot can be impressive too, although it was recently discovered that much Chilean "Merlot" was actually a different Bordeaux grape variety called Carmenère. There are a few juicy, carefully oaked Pinot Noirs around too. In general, the cheaper Chilean reds are better value than the top-of-the-range wines, which lack great complexity.

France

Any serious wine drinker will tell you that the very best French red wines still provide benchmarks for the rest of the world. Sample top red Bordeaux (claret), Burgundy, and Rhône at every opportunity and you will enjoy sublime stuff, but be prepared for the occasional expensive disappointment, especially from the first two regions, as France is still not the most reliable of winemaking countries. Even so, Bordeaux at its best offers beautifully well-balanced and well-structured, complex, long-lasting reds, while Burgundy's silky-smooth Pinot Noirs, with sensual notes of strawberry and chocolate, can be exquisite. The Rhône offers a wider variety of good buys at different price points and is known for big, hearty, spicy reds. If the scary price tags of Bordeaux and Burgundy put you off, southern France and its Languedoc-Roussillon area in particular turn out more quality, modern red wine than it used to, the best in a rich, concentrated, sun-kissed style. For lighter, raspberry-fresh, almost leafy reds, head north to the Loire Valley, splash out on premium Beaujolais Villages (not the basic versions) or give Alsace's perfumed Pinot Noir a whirl.

Italy

Much to choose from but the following are must-haves: the dense, perfumed Barolos and Barbarescos of Piedmont in northern Italy, which mellow beautifully over time, making a great match for robust red meat and game dishes. Quality, price, and vintage all vary considerably, though. First-rate reds also issue forth from Tuscany's vineyards, of course, in the shape of Chianti Classico, Brunello, Montepulciano, and others. Most Tuscan wines have a pleasing, sour-cherry acidity that makes them great with food. The ripe, modern reds of the south and Sicily are particularly appealing to lovers of New World wines – try the Negroamaro or Primitivo grape varieties for a change.

Lebanon

Just one famous winery – Chateau Musar – has put Lebanese wine on the map. The Musar red is a sophisticated, Bordeaux-like blend of (mainly) Cabernet Sauvignon with Cinsault and Carignan.

New Zealand

Not long ago, New Zealand's red wines lagged seriously
behind its famous whites. Now the rich Bordeaux blends
and smooth, fruity Pinot Noirs are getting more attention,
both from winemakers and drinkers. Try Cabernet, Merlot,
Syrah, and blends from the North Island, especially the
Hawkes Bay region, and Pinot Noir from Martinborough
and the Marlborough and Central Otago regions of the
South Island.

Portugal

Underrated reds in a plethora of styles, made from
a wide variety of local and international grapes. Dão and
Bairrada are usually tannic, powerful wines that demand
hearty food; the central and southern regions tend towards
more international styles, modern and easier to quaff.
But the Douro Valley – port country – is perhaps the
most exciting area for red table wines now, producing
generously ripe, lush, but well-structured styles.

Romania

Keep an eye open for some value-for-money Romanian
reds, especially the soft Pinot Noirs from the Dealul Mare
region in the south.

South Africa

At the premium end of the market, superb reds come
from the Cape. Typically, they are concentrated but well-
balanced, oaky Bordeaux blends, or Shiraz, or Pinotage,

often from the Stellenbosch and Paarl regions. The latest tip is the great single-varietal Merlot, or choose more elegant Pinot Noir from the cooler regions southeast of Cape Town. The cheapest Cape reds, however, can still be a serious let-down.

Spain

A remarkable range of decent red wines. Rioja is Spain's most famous red, aged in oak barrels, and at its best wonderfully mellow, with strawberry and vanilla characteristics. Go for *reserva* and *gran reserva* examples for mature (and maturer) wines. Navarra and Ribera del Duero, in the northern half of the country, also turn out some smashing, often intense, dark reds. Of the two, Ribera impresses more. Somontano, in the foothills of the Pyrenees, is an exciting place, making highly modern reds. Even the cheap, everyday vino of the central and eastern regions has improved of late and makes good party gear. Olé!

United States

There is very little impressive American wine at the cheapest end of the market, and mid-priced wines can be a bit obviously oaky and sweet. But as you head into premium territory, California's majestic, long-lived Cabernet Sauvignons, incredibly concentrated, gutsy Zinfandels, serious, plummy Merlots, and well-judged Pinot Noirs can be great. Syrah looks promising too. Oregon can produce fine Pinot Noir in good years, and

further north, Washington State's squeaky clean, purely
fruity reds are making waves, especially the Merlots.

Uruguay
Tannat is worth a whirl – this is Uruguay's speciality, a
grape which makes chewy, tannic reds. Some versions are
rough and nasty; others impress with softer, slightly tarry,
blackberry flavours.

The names

Apart from countries and grape varieties, below are some
of the wine names, often the titles of European regions,
you are most likely to encounter:

Alentejo – the huge area of southeastern Portugal, south
of Lisbon, which produces some of the country's most
exciting, modern reds.
Tip: interesting, unusual flavours from Portuguese varieties.

Barolo – Nebbiolo is the grape variety behind this classic
Italian red from the Piedmont region. Tasting notes tend
to be poetic when describing Barolo, which has a lovely,
almost floral perfume and rich, intense, tarry flavour.

Beaujolais – the fresh, cherry/berry-flavoured reds made
in Beaujolais (south of Burgundy) are usually simple, light,
and meant for early drinking. More serious examples exist
in the form of Beaujolais-Villages and, best of all, the more

structured wines of ten individual village *crus*: for example, Fleurie or Morgon. Made from the Gamay grape.

Bergerac – fresh, blackcurranty reds from the eastern edge of Bordeaux, often from the same varieties as claret.

Bourgogne – the French word for Burgundy. Basic Bourgogne Rouge can be disappointingly jammy and simple, or earthy and rustic; the best examples sleek, sensuous, and sublime. Almost all made from Pinot Noir.

Châteauneuf-du-Pape – area of the Rhône Valley between Avignon and Orange that produces generally fine, powerful reds made from a cocktail of up to thirteen different grape varieties.
Tip: pick an estate wine with the papal coat of arms in glass on the bottle.

Chianti – Tuscany's most famous red wine, based on the Sangiovese grape and tasting of red berries, with hints of tobacco, tea leaf, and sour-cherry drops. Produced in a range of styles, from lean and light to rich and full-bodied.
Tip: there are eight subzones – go for Classico or Rufina.

Claret – alternative English name for red Bordeaux.

Corbières – some of the tastiest reds in the Languedoc region of southern France. Can be gutsy, and ripe with herbal and spicy hints.

Côtes du Rhône – the Rhône's most basic reds can be boring, but occasionally an underpriced, spicy gem crops up. *Tip:* Côtes du Rhône-Villages, or more select wines from sixteen named villages, are considered superior. They are a better bet, and some are worth ageing.

Douro – Portugal's port country, where increasingly impressive red table wines are turned out.

Lambrusco – avoid the imported stuff, which is usually sweet and bland, but go to Emilia-Romagna in Italy and you'll discover dry, frothy, rather tart Lambrusco, which washes down the rich local cuisine well.

Médoc – area north of the city of Bordeaux, on the left bank of the Gironde and close to the Atlantic. Although plenty of mediocre Médoc wine is made across the region, many of the most famous estates are located in the Haut-Médoc, to the south. Here you will find the villages of Margaux, St-Julien, Pauillac, and St-Estèphe, gravelly soils, and Cabernet-based claret.
Tip: try the *crus bourgeois* wines of the Haut-Médoc for less glitzy names, but often good-value and good-quality red Bordeaux.

Navarra – up-and-coming region of northern Spain, near Rioja, which produces mainly admirable reds made from Tempranillo, Cabernet, and Merlot.
Tip: quality a little patchy, so choose your producer with care.

Navarra – up-and-coming region of northern Spain, near Rioja, which produces mainly admirable reds made from Tempranillo, Cabernet, and Merlot.
Tip: quality a little patchy, so choose your producer with care.

Ribera del Duero – another quality red wine region of Spain, with several star estates, the most famous being Vega Sicilia. Big, solid, concentrated wines, usually from Tempranillo (often called Tinto del País in Spain) or Tempranillo with Cabernet and/or Garnacha.

St-Emilion – Bordeaux appellation on the Right Bank of the Gironde with a beautiful ancient hilltop town and myriad small winemakers rather than big châteaux. Merlot dominates the blend, which tend to be more fleshy and soft than other clarets.

Valpolicella – basic "Valpol" from Italy's Veneto region is light and insubstantial, but top examples have more depth and a moreish, sour-cherry character. Do try very powerful, dense Recioto (sweet) and Amarone (dry) della Valpolicella, made from the concentrated juice of dried grapes.

Vin de Pays d'Oc – wine from anywhere in the warm Languedoc-Roussillon region of southern France, many of which are ripe and fulsome, oaky and modern. The best are the Cabernets, Syrahs, and Syrah blends (*see* overleaf).

Getting wine wise

What is corked wine?

This has nothing to do with a crumbly cork that leaves bits in your wine! It means that a mould-affected, natural-bark cork has tainted the wine, giving it a musty aroma and cardboard flavour (some liken it to mushrooms). The problem is all too common. If you think you have bought a corked bottle, take it back to the shop (or alert a waiter in a restaurant) and ask for a replacement. Wines sealed with plastic corks or screw caps never suffer from cork taint, but bear in mind that they may not age as well.

What are vin de pays?

A class of French wine designed in 1973 to create a new category between basic *vin de table* (table wine) and the much more strictly regulated *appellation contrôlée* (AC) wines. The idea was that more producers would strive to achieve higher standards and that mavericks working outside AC strictures would get more recognition. Today, *vins de pays* are often the most modern, New World-like French wines of all, although styles run the gamut from the light, perfumed dry whites of the Vin de Pays du Jardin de la France (Loire area) to the big, oaky reds of the Vin de Pays d'Oc (Languedoc). And so many exist that it's hard to comment on the general quality, although many are impressive and well-priced.

The countries

Argentina

Argentinian Chardonnay is generally very pleasant stuff, ripe, modern, and oaky. One or two great examples exist, and many others have potential.

white wines a–z

Australia

A lot of wine drinkers discovered modern, fruit-forward, New World whites in the shape of Aussie Chardonnay or Chardonnay/Semillon blends. You know the ones: all soft pineapple and peach flavours and lots of vanilla or buttery oak. Today, whites in this style come from all over the winemaking globe and, frankly, they can get pretty boring. Ring the changes by trying more interesting Australian white wines. There's much to choose from: toasty Hunter Valley Semillon produced north of Sydney, or lime-rich Clare and Eden Valley Riesling from South Australia. Nutty Verdelhos, and rich, peachy Marsannes or Viogniers are rarer, but worth tracking down. And more elegant, subtly oaked or unoaked Chardonnays from cool-climate regions such as the Yarra Valley, Tasmania, and Adelaide Hills are starting to cause a stir. Fans of Sauvignon Blanc might find the odd gem from cool, high-altitude regions, but this is not Australia's ace card.

Austria

They are not terribly well-known in the outside world,
but Austria's Rieslings and Grüner Veltliners (a local grape)
can be thrilling: bone-dry with spine-tingling acidity
and wonderfully refreshing flavours of lemon, grapefruit,
and white pepper. Some sturdier, oaky Chardonnays are
also produced there (Austrians sometimes call this grape
"Morillon"), and racy Sauvignon Blanc is made in Styria.
High standards of winemaking are common.

Bulgaria

The softly oaked, easy-drinking style of Bulgarian
Chardonnay, plus its relatively low price tag, make it a
great buy, even though (or, perhaps, precisely because) it
is so unfashionable. Other white wines from Bulgaria are
too often a disappointment to recommend at present.

Canada

Rare as hen's teeth outside North America, but Canadian
Chardonnays and Rieslings from the major wine-producing
states of British Columbia and Ontario can be deeply
impressive, well-crafted and long-lived, with crisp acidity.

Chile

Just as its Cabernets, Merlots, and Pinots provide some
of the best middle-market reds around, so Chile's
Chardonnays – and, to a lesser extent, its Sauvignon Blancs
– give us some of the most attractive whites available at
reasonably low prices. The Chardonnays are reliable, with

lovely, fresh, tropical fruit and judicious use of oak, but
avoid the top-of-the range ones, which don't compete
as well with the best of France and the New World. The
Sauvignons from cool-climate areas like Casablanca, can
be zippy, crisp, and aromatic. A few decent, perfumed
Gewurztraminers exist too.

England

The problem with English white wine is its price, as
there are few economies of scale. That said, some recent
bottlings, often made with obscure grape varieties, can
be delicate and attractive, smelling of meadow grass
and blossom, and tasting of lemons and apples.

France

As with its reds, the very best white wines from France
are world-beaters. When you sample a brilliant white
Burgundy – a splendidly rich tapestry of bright fruit, nuts,
and fine oak – it is the apogee of premium Chardonnay. The
top Sancerres and Pouilly-Fumés are exquisitely elegant yet
steely, mineral-drenched expressions of Sauvignon Blanc.
Then there's top white Bordeaux, a beautiful balancing act
between lean Sauvignon and fatter Semillon; richly peachy
Viognier from the Rhône; and the honeyed, nutty flavours
of the best Chenin Blanc in the world from Vouvray. And
no list of great French whites would be complete without
the exotically spicy, aromatic, food-friendly wines of Alsace
in the far east. If you want to start with more humble
offerings, try the *vins de pays* from around the country

(*see* page 33). A word of warning: the cheapest white *vins de table* – the ones you pick up for virtually nothing in French hypermarkets – are still mostly vile.

Germany

German Riesling is much underrated. This is naturally light, subtle, yet long-lived and complex white wine that smells and tastes of blossom, fresh, tangy apples and oranges when young, and honey with (strangely) a whiff of petrol, when mature. It's fantastic stuff and often very reasonably priced – even the older vintages. Other grape varieties are grown in Germany, of which the grapefruit-flavoured Scheurebe is a personal favourite, but Riesling is really what it is all about. Renounce all pretenders such as the lily-livered and pathetic Liebfraumilch in favour of something that says "Riesling" on the label.

Greece

Retsina is the best-known Greek white, a resinous, pine-scented oddity that most either loathe or, well, quite like. Some modern, new-wave Greek whites are just starting to appear on the market, including some commendable Chardonnays. Look out for them.

Hungary

A few good-value Hungarian whites can be found, mainly on supermarket shelves. The best are snappy Sauvignon Blanc, Gewurztraminer, and a local grape called Irsai Oliver, all made in a dry, aromatic, rather savoury style.

Italy

Oceans of Pinot Grigio, Orvieto, Frascati, and Soave
are lapped up by the world every year, but these wines
are almost always bland, unless you pick the top producers.
Other Italian whites can be more interesting: sample
the fruity Arneis and nutty Favorita grapes of Piedmont;
the racy, crisp whites of Trentino and Alto Adige; refreshing
Lugana from Lake Garda; or Tuscany's excellent
Chardonnays. Even the once old-fashioned wineries of the
south and Sicily have made rapid progress and turn out
great-value modern whites in a ripe, fruit-forward style.

New Zealand

The exuberant, pungent Sauvignon Blancs of Marlborough
on New Zealand's South Island have made a major impact
on international markets. Quite right too: these intense
wines with their blast of gooseberry, asparagus, grass,
and white currant are as striking as white wine ever gets,
even if you tire of their loud character after a while. South
Island Chardonnay is pure and fruity with a crisp, clean
character, but becomes more exotic, ripe, and tropical
from the warmer North. Riesling and Gewurztraminer
can be ultra-fresh, zippy, and fragrant from cooler spots,
and do look out for up-and-coming Pinot Gris.

Portugal

Vinho Verde, drunk ever-so fresh, young, and faintly spritzy,
has a simple, thirst-quenching appeal. But the winemakers
of the central and southern regions are now making more

modern styles, interestingly from local grape varieties more often than the ubiquitous Chardonnay. Worth a punt.

South Africa

The Cape is probably better known for its reds, but the Chardonnays in particular can be stunning, whether they are rich and assertive ones from warmer regions or more restrained examples from cooler spots. Sauvignon Blanc has come on greatly in recent years and seems to hit a nice balance between Loire and New Zealand styles. A few impressive Semillons exist too. Chenin Blanc is the workhorse grape, and many cheap Chenins are good for party plonk, although a few more serious examples exist.

Spain

Traditional oak-aged white Rioja is big on vanilla, sawdust, and cream – a style most either love or loathe. More modern, international styles of white Rioja are now emerging, although you might think they miss the point. Elsewhere, some bang-up-to-date, fruity Chardonnays are made in Somontano and Navarra – racy dry Sauvignons and Verdejos in Rueda in the northwest. The most tempting whites, however, come from Galicia, in the far northwest of the country, in the form of weighty (but not oaky) Albariño, with a fruity, peach-and-lime character. Brilliant with fish.

USA

Top California Chardonnays are rightly revered for their balance between ripe fruit and hefty oak. Some cooler-climate spots are coming up with more restrained, crisper examples. Cheap West Coast Chardonnays, however, can be too commercial, in a sweetish, over-oaked way. Sauvignon Blanc has improved a great deal from the days when it was always made in a flabby, Fumé Blanc style. Some rich, perfumed Viognier is now available and should be sampled. Oregon's Pinot Gris is patchy, but when on form, it's superb, and Washington State's highly fruity, clean Chardonnays and Semillons are worth a whirl – although, again, avoid the cheapies.

The names

Bianco di Custoza – low-priced, gluggable Italian white from near Verona, with a lemon-sherbet character.

Chablis – region of northern Burgundy famous for its Chardonnay, which traditionally has been steelier and more mineral than examples made further south. Riper, richer examples are now emerging.

Condrieu – headily perfumed, richly concentrated whites made from peachy Viognier in the Rhône.
Tip: quality varies but prices are nearly always sky-high. Choose carefully.

Entre-Deux-Mers – Bordeaux appellation making zesty, fresh dry whites from the Sauvignon Blanc and Semillon grape varieties.

Frascati – Italian white wine made in the Lazio area near Rome. Light, easy-drinking, rather bland stuff.
Tip: it's worth seeking out a top producer and paying a little more.

Liebfraumilch – insipid, off-dry German white, mainly made from the dull Müller-Thurgau grape. Fell out of fashion in the 1990s as fruitier New World wines took hold.

Meursault – some of Burgundy's most highly regarded whites are made around this village in the Côte d'Or. Rich, gold-coloured Chardonnays with creamy, nutty layers.

Mosel-Saar-Ruwer – German Riesling is never so delightfully delicate, floral, appley or honeyed as when it comes from the vineyards of the Mosel.
Tip: pick up mature examples of fine wines at amazingly low prices.

Muscadet – the crisp, faintly yeasty, dry white of the Loire Valley around Nantes makes a good match for seafood.
Tip: basic Muscadet lacks character, but go for one that says *sur lie* on the label to taste the extra creaminess that comes from lees ageing.

Orvieto – Italian white from Umbria, usually fresh and dry, if a bit bland.
Tip: the Classico zone produces rather better, fuller-flavoured wines.

Pouilly-Fumé – some of the Loire's best Sauvignon Blancs are made in this appellation. Wines are bone-dry and lemony and have a characteristic pungency which some liken to gun-flint and smoke (hence *fumé*, French for smoked). Can be overpriced.

Retsina – Greece's resinous whites have a pine-tree smell and rather oily flavour. Losing ground to more modern Greek wines at home and abroad.

Sancerre – another Loire appellation turning out fine Sauvignon Blanc, very dry and tangy. Like Pouilly-Fumé, prices can be too high but quality is more consistent.

Soave – Italian Soave, made near Verona, is generally rather mundane stuff, although one or two gifted producers manage to inject some riper, lemon-and-almond character into the wine.
Tip: pay extra for the best labels.

Vin de Pays des Côtes de Gascogne – racy, refreshing, grassy whites usually made from a blend of Ugni Blanc and Colombard in Southwest France.
Tip: good-value party white.

Vinho Verde – northwest Portugal's white wine is sometimes sulphurous and flat, although perfumed, clean, slightly spritzy examples are a delight.
Tip: drink young with oily fish.

Vouvray – Chenin Blanc both blissful and bog-standard from the Loire. White Vouvray is made dry, medium, and sweet. Good wines should have an appley freshness and notes of walnut and, with age, honey.

Getting wine wise

Which whites in winter?
Think "seasonally" when choosing white wines. It simply doesn't work to sip ice-cold Vinho Verde around the fireplace in December, despite the fact that you fell in love with the style on holiday in July. Richer, fuller-flavoured whites such as oaked Chardonnays or perfumed Viogniers seem better-suited to cold nights. If you don't like powerful, buttery whites, simply turn up the volume to something fruitier, moving, say, from grassy, light French Sauvignon to one from New Zealand. Bigger wines go with heartier, "cold weather", grub too.

How to get good advice?
Ask for help in a wine shop or restaurant; there should be someone around who can answer questions about wine (and if not, go elsewhere!) Find out: which "bin ends" are on special offer; what's new; whether the dry sherries or rosés are fresh stock; what matches your dinner dish; what a particular wine tastes like; etc. Why not ask to try something that you intend to buy in bulk? Finally, always return a dud bottle (corked, oxidized, generally sub-standard). Demand more from those who sell us our wine!

The countries

Australia
Some typically big and ripe, gutsy rosés are made Down Under, mainly from Grenache. Alcohol levels are higher than usual and there is plenty of rich red-berry flavour. *Tip:* these more powerful styles can age a little longer than lighter European rosés.

rosé wines a–z

California
Avoid the pale, sweetish, so-called "white" or "blush" Zinfandels, which tend to be wimpy, and go for new-wave, dark-pink, vibrantly fruity West Coast rosés, especially those made from Syrah.

France
Reject the inexplicably popular but fruitless Rosé d'Anjou, made from the boring Grolleau grape, in favour of better raspberry and grass-scented Loire pinks such as Cabernet d'Anjou and Rosé de Loire – these are mainly Cabernet Franc. And don't miss the Syrah and Grenache rosés from the southern Rhône and deep south for richer flavours of rosehips, redcurrants, and a hint of creamy toffee. Those from Tavel and Provence can be full and ripe, and so stand up well to Mediterranean fish dishes, cold meat, and garlic.

Italy

Italian *rosato*, as it's called, can be excellent: fresh and
well-balanced, relatively light and crisp from the north;
fuller and riper from central regions and further south.
Tip: Carmignano, northwest of Florence, makes some tasty
dry pinks, as does Cirò – part of the Calabria region.

Portugal

Once famous for the spritzy, off-dry, and insipid Mateus
Rosé, now producing a few more modern, fruit-driven pinks.

Spain

Bright, vibrant Spanish *rosado* is about as moreish as wine
ever gets. The best come from Navarra and Rioja and have
a lively cherry-and-strawberry character. They are usually
made from Grenache. Try one with a plate of cold *jamón*.

Getting wine wise

Staying in the pink...

Always, but always, chill rosé wines, still or sparkling,
to emphasize their fresh, crisp, succulent qualities. Still
versions are rather fragile wines; their summer-berry
flavours and aromas don't last long, so drink them while
they're youthful to enjoy them at their best. The light,
mouth-watering, tangy style of most rosé makes it
particularly suitable for hot summer days – the ideal
lunchtime wine, especially with cold meats, prawns,
or salty tapas.

The countries

Austria
Sekt made from Riesling and Pinot Blanc can be fair quality
– racy and clean – although you'll probably have to go
there to try it.

sparkling wines a–z

Australia
Cheap and cheerful Aussie sparklers abound, and these can
be good value, if rather simple. Expect big bubbles and
tutti-frutti flavours. More serious and impressive sparklers
are made by the traditional Champagne method from cool-
climate fruit. The best come from Tasmania and Victoria's
Yarra Valley and are made from a blend of Chardonnay and
Pinot Noir. Don't miss Australia's red sparklers, either –
they are peppery, rich, and ruddy. Most are made from the
Shiraz grape. Fun fizz, especially at Christmas time.

California
The West Coast makes some of the most sophisticated
and finely tuned sparklers around, but they're not cheap.
The cooler spots – Anderson County, Carneros – produce
the higher-acid Pinot Noir and Chardonnay required for
elegant fizz. Some of the best are made by Californian
wineries that are owned by Champagne houses.

England

Bubbly is currently England's most promising style of wine – some vineyards enjoy a similar climate and soil as Champagne, after all, and they produce the lean, tart base wine needed for zippy fizz. Grapes vary, but the most exciting *cuvées* are made from Chardonnay and Pinot Noir. Try them if you get the chance.

France

Champagne can be sublime, a wonderful balancing act between crisp acidity, refined fruit flavours, small-beaded mousse and richer, creamy, bready notes. On the other hand, it can be a huge let-down, lean and tart with little discernible character. Avoid the very cheapest non-vintage Champagnes, don't drink vintage too early, and best of all, find a reliable brand you like and stick with it. This is a rare instance when the big brands tend to be among the best.

Champagne is usually a blend of three grapes: Chardonnay, Pinot Noir, and Pinot Meunier. However, Champagne *blanc de blancs* is one hundred per cent Chardonnay – at its best elegant, with yellow-fruit (pineapples, lemons) flavour, and a creamy quality. Champagne *blanc de noirs* (literally "white from black") is made entirely from the clear juice of the black grapes Pinots Noir and Meunier. These bubblies tend to be aromatic and relatively full-bodied.

Pink Champagne is not just a gimmick. Sure, it looks pretty, but it also tastes fruitier, with red-berry and yoghurt flavour and a summery scent of fresh raspberries. Try brut (dry) Champagnes with light seafood, fish, or vegetable canapés; demi-sec (sweeter) examples with fresh fruit and mousses, jellies, and fools; and pink Champagne with subtly spiced Oriental food and sushi. Absolutely fabulous!

Outside Champagne, avoid really cheap French fizz at all costs and instead try crémant, a newish class of fizz designed to offer premium sparklers. Crémant is made in the same manner as Champagne, but sometimes from different varieties, and it's usually cheaper. Sparkling wine from the Loire can be particularly patchy in quality. Choose a reputable producer and it's worth a foray – some fizzy Saumurs and Vouvrays (made from Chenin Blanc) are snappy, refreshing, and appley.

Tip: try Crémant d'Alsace and Crémant de Bourgogne.

Germany

Sekt (made from Riesling, Pinot Blanc, or inferior grapes) is often a disappointment. A typical example is cheap, but not particularly good quality, with angular acidity.

Italy

The most famous Italian sparkler is Asti, a sweet, frothy, low-alcohol fizz that's refreshing with pudding but no great shakes otherwise. Its cousin Moscato d'Asti is better, fresh and as sweet as crunchy green grapes dusted with icing sugar. If you prefer a drier style, try crisp, sherbetty Prosecco from the hills around Treviso, near Venice.

New Zealand

The sparkling wines made in Marlborough, on the South Island, are, almost without exception, excellent – pure, clean, and lemony, with fresh acidity.
Tip: medium-priced and hard to beat for value.

South Africa

Méthode Cap Classique is the term used to describe wines from the Cape made in the traditional Champagne method. Some of them have admirable finesse and style, but they are still a rare sight on the export market.

Spain

Spanish cava, from Penedès in eastern Spain, is super stuff, providing everyday bubbly at affordable prices. Expect a fairly neutral style, with appley freshness and sometimes an earthy note. A blend of local grapes – Xarel-lo, Parellada, and Macabeo – although some modern, fruitier *cuvées* embrace Chardonnay too.

Getting wine wise

Anyone for aperitifs?

Sparkling wine has high acidity which makes it a perfect aperitif. Other apt aperitifs include fino and manzanilla sherries, bone-dry Sauvignon, and appley Riesling. Chill all aperitifs before serving.

The countries

Australia

Liqueur Muscat is an Australian speciality, produced in the Rutherglen region of Victoria. Liquid raisins, with notes of spice, toffee, and fruit cake, this is warming, hearty stuff.

sweet & fortified a–z

France

Golden, honeyed, fortified Muscats with a floral scent and fresh finish appear from southern France in the form of *vins doux naturels*. The most famous is Muscat de Beaumes-de-Venise, closely followed by Muscats from Rivesaltes and Frontignan. Try sweet red Banyuls too, from Grenache. Some of the most opulent and majestic sweet wines in the world are made in Sauternes and Barsac around Bordeaux, where botrytis rot affects the Semillon and Sauvignon grapes. Monbazillac is a cheaper alternative. And in the Loire, beautifully crisp yet sweet wines are created with Chenin Blanc.

Germany

Great dessert wines, with fresh, crisp acidity to balance the sweetness, made from late harvest and nobly rotten grapes. The best are Rieslings; the sweetest are *Eisweins*, made from the concentrated juice of winter-picked, semi-frozen grapes.

Hungary

Tokáji, the "dessert wine of kings", is one of the most wonderful wines in the world. Made mainly from the Furmint grape, it tastes of candied peel, toffee, marmalade.

Italy

Produces the fabulous Vin Santo: a luscious, barley-sugar and nuts sweetie made from dried grapes.

Portugal

The land of port, which hails from the upper Douro Valley in the north. Here, red grapes bake on steep vineyard slopes and produce (in great years) the powerful, headily rich vintage port, which takes years to mature. Lesser styles include late-bottled vintage (LBV), from not-so-good years, and single *quinta*, from one estate. These can provide excellent value. A personal favourite is tawny port, long-aged in oak barrels for a mellow, nutty style that's delicious lightly chillled. And don't forget Madeira, the fortified, "cooked" (heated) wine from the island of the same name.

Spain

The land of sherry. The area around Jerez in southern Spain, produces white wine from the Palomino grape, which is then affected by a natural yeast coating called *flor* that gives it a salty tang. Pale, dry, crisp fino and manzanilla are the result. Oxidized/aged versions are known as amontillado (usually medium-dry) and oloroso (richer, older and often sweeter, although do look out for rare but delectably dry.)

storing & serving wine

Is it important to store and serve wine correctly? If you are going to drink a wine within hours of buying it, store it anyway you like. If, however, you intend to keep it for some days or weeks, it pays to know how certain factors may affect its character. As for serving – well, you can always neck it from the bottle on the way home, but that's not going to do justice to fine wine. A few hints, then, on showing your wine in its very best light....

Don't make the mistake of thinking that all wines improve
with age. Many inexpensive wines should be enjoyed as quickly
as possible after bottling. Leave them around for too long and
their fragile fruit flavours and freshness disappear quickly.
That's why some wines you enjoy on your summer holidays
taste dreadful by Christmas. Most labels don't offer a clue as
to whether a wine will improve or fade away with keeping, so
it's helpful to have an idea of which styles will last the course.

wines that will improve

Wines that won't improve over time
* Almost all rosés, especially light, delicate examples. The
deepest rosés keep the best, but in general, drink up pink!
* Neutral, insubstantial whites with little character. Try
keeping a cheap Frascati or Muscadet for long and you'll
soon find out why you shouldn't.
* Soft, juicy, jammy reds with little structure. Basic
Beaujolais, for example, should never be cellared.
* Inexpensive fizz and light non-vintage Champagne.
Be spontaneous and crack it open, now!
* Dry fino and manzanilla sherry. Drink up soon to capture
that fresh, almost salty character.

Wines that will keep for a year or so
* Ripe, fruity whites such as New World Chardonnay and
Sauvignon should retain their character for several months.

* Medium-bodied, well-balanced reds can cellar well for a year or so, simply softening a little.
* Rioja Reserva and Gran Reserva. The ageing has been done in the *bodega* (winery), so don't hang on to it for ever.
* The best non-vintage Champagnes and premium sparklers. Good acidity and depth of flavour mean they benefit if stored for a short while.

Wines that improve with age

* Fine German and Austrian Rieslings become honeyed and even petrolly.
* Australian Semillon and Riesling. A few years in bottle bring richer, lime-marmalade depths.
* Any rich, tannic, powerful red (premium red Bordeaux, Rhône, New World Cabernet and Shiraz .) These soften and mellow with age, emerging smoother and more rounded.
* Fine dessert wines from Austria, Canada, France, Germany, and Hungary become more luscious and opulent and lose sharp acidity as they mature.
* Chenin Blanc from the Loire Valley. Dry, medium, or sweet, the best examples need lots of time to open up and soften.
* Vintage Champagne is often released too early. Preferably drink at least ten years after vintage.
* Vintage port needs a long time to settle down, loosen up, and release complex, deep flavours and aromas.

Lay your wine down

If you are keeping a bottle for more than a week or two, store it on its side. This means the liquid is in contact with the cork, keeping it plump and tight in the neck of the bottle. If you stand the bottle upright, the cork dries out in time, shrinks, and lets in air. The result? Oxidized wine.

For those lucky enough to have a cellar in their home, wine storage will present no problems. A cellar is usually the perfect place to store wine: dark, secluded, still, vaguely damp and cool.

storing wine at home

How long to keep once open?

Once opened and exposed to the air, wine oxidizes and deteriorates, similar to when a cut apple turns brown. Light, delicate table wines should be enjoyed within two days of opening, while rich, robust ones may be OK after three or even four. Ports and sherries taste fine for a couple of weeks after opening, sometimes longer, and Madeira keeps for months. Always re-seal the bottle between servings and store in a cool, dark place.

Why does it need to be all those things? Darkness is important, as constant bright light gradually affects the character of a wine. Still and secluded count too – not only because glass bottles are fragile, but also because motion affects wine, so store it away from vibrations and knocks. Cool is crucial. If wine is stored at a warm temperature – or worse, at constantly fluctuating temperatures – it will quickly deteriorate. Ideally, keep it at a steady, slightly chilly 7–10°C (45–50°F). Some humidity is preferable to absolute dryness too, as it will stop the cork from drying out. And keep the bottles away from strong smells such as white spirit, petrol, or pongy paints, as they can alter wine for the worse.

If you don't have a cellar, try to find a space in your house where as many of the above conditions apply.

Good spots: the space under the stairs; an old cupboard in a quiet corner; a dark and disused fireplace; even under the bed (a non-vibrating one, preferably...)

Bad spots: the garage or utility room (fluctuating temperatures and strong smells); the greenhouse or garden shed (too cold in winter, hot in summer); the kitchen (too warm at times); the utility room (hot, juddering machines); or anywhere near a functioning boiler or heater.

Creating a storage space for wine

* Try to insulate the spot you have chosen against cold draughts, and turn off any radiators.
* If the room is very dry, keep a bowl of water or a damp sponge in there to add moisture to the air.
* Keep bottles lying on their sides so that the corks don't dry out. Either leave them in their original boxes, or store them on wine racks (wooden ones are better than metal ones, which can tear the labels.)
* Consider the security of valuable wine.

Finally, if you are storing lots of wine, it's sensible to keep cellar notes to remind you when you bought each batch and when it might be ready to drink. If in doubt, open and pour your wine. It is there to be enjoyed, not squirrelled away in the dark for ever!

There are loads of fancy corkscrews on the market, but note how many wine waiters still stick with the most simple "waiter's friend" version. Take your pick, but remember that you don't have to spend a fortune on the latest designer model.

opening the bottle

Remove a cork carefully, especially if it is crumbly. And if the wine has thrown a sediment, handle the bottle with care so that you don't disturb it too much; pour gently, throwing away the muddy dregs.

Open sparkling wine and Champagne with great caution. Shaking a bottle of fizz until it explodes is dangerous and wasteful. Never point a Champagne bottle at someone's face. Instead, direct it at a wall, with your hand over it as you remove the wire cage, and aim to ease the cork out with a soft "pssht", twisting the bottle in one hand and the cork in another. Use a dry cloth to hold damp bottles firmly.

Temperature

Wine is often served too warm or too cold. To get it right:
* Chill all whites, sparklers, rosés, and dry, pale sherries for at least an hour, preferably two, before serving. Don't chill them *too* long or their flavours and aromas will be muted.
* Serve light, soft, juicy reds at a cool room temperature or chill them very slightly to bring out their tangy character.

* Rich, tannic reds should be served at room temperature.
* Serve sweet, rich sherries at room temperature. Likewise
ripe, red ports; but a mellow tawny is delicious lightly chilled.

Decanting

The benefits of opening a bottle an hour or two before
serving to "let it breathe" are overrated. Tough, tightly
knit wine (we're talking reds and ports here) does soften
and mellow when exposed to air, but only a very little bit
is in contact with the outside world unless you pour it
out. Use a glass decanter for this, or simply swirl the wine
around vigorously in big glasses at the table. A decanter
is also useful for separating the sediment thrown by some
rich reds and ports. Stand the bottle upright for a day or
two to let the deposit settle. Pour the liquid slowly and
carefully into the decanter until you start to see sediment
in the wine. A bright light behind the bottle may help here.

Glasses

The very best glasses for showing off fine wine are plain,
clear, and simple (so you can examine the wine's colour and
texture easily.) They have a long stem, so you can hold them
there, rather than getting hot, sticky fingers round the bowl,
and they tend to be large, so you can swirl the wine around,
releasing its aroma. Don't fill to the brim, but leave enough
space for sloshing the liquid around without spilling it. The
ideal Champagne glasses are tall, slim flutes, for creating
long streams of bubbles, and the best vessels for sherry
are not stingy schooners, but normal white wine glasses.

Temperature in restaurants

Reds are often served
much too warm in
restaurants – send your
bottle of hot jam back or
ask for an ice bucket to
cool it down. Any waiter
worth his/her salt should
understand that warm
wine is unacceptable. The
best restaurants should
offer Beaujolais and other
light reds lightly chilled.
Likewise, don't put up with
whites, fizz, or rosés that
haven't been chilled, and
expect the waiter to come
up with a way of keeping
them cool once opened
(ice bucket, fridge).
Demand to have your
wine served correctly,
just like your food!

Where do you go from here? Armed with new knowledge about the subject of wine, it pays to move on, perhaps to some different ways to shop for the stuff. And remember to taste as much wine as you possibly can.

moving on

Wine accessories

Wine thermometers, fancy stoppers, and silver ice buckets (not to mention vine-embossed hankies) might make jolly gifts for the wine buff, but there are only three wine-related gadgets that are essential: a decent corkscrew, a simple foil cutter, and a cooling sleeve. The sleeve lives in the freezer and can be popped round a bottle of white to cool it down in minutes – less ostentatious, and less messy, than an ice bucket.

Buying wine in supermarkets is easy, and many stock a huge range. But they are never hugely inspiring places, and the staff are rarely genned up. The major high street off-licence chains can be more exciting spots to purchase interesting bottles, but if your local is bigger on beer and ciggies than vino, then look elsewhere.

Try an independent merchant – these kinds of wine shops tend to have a more eclectic and exciting selection. And they often hire staff who know more about the range. Spend some time in the shop chatting with an assistant about what you are after.

A specialist – if you've discovered a love for, say, Austrian wines, or top red Burgundy, track down a specialist in the field who can offer you a wider range. A consumer wine magazine may help, or ask any wine-buff friends.

Mail order – this is a great idea, in that wine is a heavy and difficult commodity to lug around. Again, think about

choosing an independent merchant, and always go for
a well-established one with a helpful, inspiring catalogue.

The internet – there are now several well-known wine
merchants selling over the internet. Surf away – I
recommend using a known and trusted name rather than
a small, obscure company. A good website should give you
loads of information about wine in general, and about the
bottles you intend to buy in particular. If possible, do check
prices against supermarket/off-licence ones for similar
labels before buying.

Auction houses – a number of fine-wine connoisseurs still
buy at auction, whether for drinking or investment. I can't
help saying that I believe wine is for enjoying, not making
a profit on, but to track down a parcel of seriously good,
mature wine and bid for it can be a thrill.

Reading and tasting

If you want to learn more, read about wine as much
as you can (do use new, up-to-date books, as the wine
world changes all the time), but don't forget there is no
substitute for tasting. Take every opportunity to sample
as many wines as possible, and make a few notes if it
will help you remember what you liked or loathed.

Finally, never be swayed by someone else's opinion if
a wine seems better or worse to you. It's your palate
that counts when choosing wine, so stick to your guns!

Tips on cleaning glasses

Wash wine glasses by
hand in very hot water,
and avoid using detergent,
if possible, especially if
serving sparkling wine,
as the smallest trace of
soap can make a fizz go
flat. If you must use
washing-up liquid, rinse
the glasses afterwards
extra thoroughly. Dry and
polish with a clean, soft
cotton or linen cloth.
Store them away carefully
where they won't get
dusty or greasy and give
them another quick polish
before using next time.

glossary

Appellation Contrôlée (AC/AOC) French wines made to the strictest standards, with rules governing grapes, soils, yields, alcohol, and vineyard souce. Generally a sign of premium quality wine, although there are exceptions.

Barrique A 225-litre oak barrel, used to ferment/age wine.

Brut "Dry." Seen on Champagne and sparkling wine labels.

Classico Italian term denoting that a wine – for example, Chianti or Soave – has been made in (supposedly) the best part of the designated zone.

Crianza Spanish wine that has been barrel-aged for one year. *Sin crianza* means "unoaked".

Cru Literally "growth" in French. Refers to a single estate or property, or a specific, usually highly rated, vineyard area. *Cru classé* is a growth from the Medoc's five-tier classification system. *Grand cru* is the top category of named vineyard site; *premier cru* the second highest.

Cuvée A simple way of referring to a batch of wine. A Champagne house might make a dry non-vintage *cuvée* and a special anniversary *cuvée*. A New World producer is more likely to use the term bin, as in bin number.

Demi-sec Medium-sweet.

DO/DOC/DOCG Refers to wines made under controls, less strict for DO but more so for DOC and DOCG in Portugal, Spain, and Italy (DOCG is Italian only). As for AC, a general indication of quality premium wine, but no guarantee.

Late harvest/vendange tardive Sweeter, riper-tasting wine than usual made from grapes harvested later than the normal time. These are sometimes botrytized (nobly rotten).

Méthode traditionnelle The Champagne method of making sparkling wine, widely considered the best.

Mis en bouteille par... French term meaning "bottled by...".

Nouveau New wine, usually very light and simple, just released from a recent vintage. Meant to be drunk young.

Qualitätswein Means "quality wine" in German, but don't expect all bottles marked thus to please. QbA (*bestimmter Anbaugebeit*) indicates premium wine made in a specific region of Germany, while QmP (*mit Prädikat*) has a special quality based on sugar levels.

Quinta Portuguese farm or estate.

Reserve/reserva/riserva "Reserve" has no legal meaning in France. In Spain, Portugal, and Italy however, it refers to wines that have spent longer ageing before release. Often the best wines are kept back for barrel-ageing. *Gran reserva* (usually Spain) means even longer in cask/bottle.

Sec/secco/seco "Dry".

Sur lie Aged on the yeast sediment (lees) and bottled directly from it, without racking or filtering.

Trocken German term for "dry".

Vin de pays *See* page 33.

Vin de table/vin de mesa/vinho de mesa/vino da tavola Basic table wine from, respectively, France, Spain, Portugal, and Italy. Quality often ranges from ordinary to poor, but you might come across the odd gem.

index